To . . . .

From . .

OTHER MINI GIFTBOOKS IN THIS SERIES:

Welcome to the New Baby
To a very special Aunt
To a very special Daughter
To a very special Grandmother
To a very special Mother-in-law
To a very special Grandpa
Happy Anniversary
To my very special Love
To a very special Mother
To a very special Son
To a very special Dad

To a very special Friend
To a very special Granddaughter
Wishing you Happiness
To my very special Husband
Merry Christmas
To a very special Sister
To my very special Wife
To someone special Happy
    Birthday
To someone very special Happy
    Birthday

Published simultaneously in 1998 by Exley Publications LLC in the
USA and Exley Publications Ltd in Great Britain.

12 11 10 9 8 7 6 5 4 3 2 1

Copyright © Helen Exley 1998
ISBN 1-86187-011-6

Edited and words selected by Helen Exley, with main messages
written by Pam Brown.
Illustrated by Juliette Clarke
Printed and bound in Hungary

Exley Publications Ltd, 16 Chalk Hill, Watford, Herts WD1 4BN, UK.
Exley Publications LLC, 232 Madison Avenue, Suite 1206,
NY 10016, USA.

ACKNOWLEDGEMENTS: The publishers are grateful for permission to reproduce copyright
material. Whilst every reasonable effort has been made to trace copyright holders, the
publishers would be pleased to hear from any not here acknowledged. EILEEN CADDY: Used
with permission of Findhorn Press. ELEANOR ROOSEVELT: From You Learn By Living,
published by HarperCollins Inc. © 1960 E. Roosevelt, renewed 1988, Franklin A. Roosevelt.
MARGARET SLOAN-HUNTER: From "Passing", from A Portrait of American Mothers and
Daughters published by NewSage Press 1987. Pam Brown, Charlotte Gray, Peter Gray and
Helen Thomson © Helen Exley, 1998.

Wishing you

THE BEST BIRTHDAY EVER

Edited by Helen Exley
Illustrated by Juliette Clarke

It's birthday time! So fill the cup
of life to the brim. Relax,
have fun, and may the year
ahead be full of love and friendship.

. . .

A HELEN EXLEY GIFTBOOK

EXLEY
NEW YORK • WATFORD, UK

HAPPY BIRTHDAY!

May this day be a day to remember.

And may the coming year bring you new hopes,

new beginnings, new adventures, new discoveries.

...

I wish you discoveries and marvels. I wish you

success. I wish you joy and peace and deep

contentment. And always, always, love.

...

May you find the work, the friends, the
opportunities and the love you long for.
Meet the future with hope and courage, enthusiasm,
energy and joy. Take them all and from them build a
life that's worth the living.

…

May your eyes see even more clearly.
May your ears hear even more subtly.
May your mouth speak even more wisely.
May your nose sniff splendid things
– the sea and roses, new bread, fresh tar, the
scent of the seasons.
May your touch bring kindliness and comfort.
May your mind revel in exploration.

…

May you never cease to search and challenge. May
you always find something to delight you. May you
always have joy in living.

…

PARTY TIME!

This is Your Day. This is Your Time.

Dress it up in spangles.

Time enough ahead to be non-stop sensible.

Just think – one day you will want a quiet

dinner at home on your birthday.

Candlelight. A couple of bottles of wine. Soft music.

Pleasant conversation.

One day.

...

There's always room for the ridiculous

– especially on birthdays.

If you can't dance and laugh and do daft things *now*

– when on earth *are* you to do them?

...

A job, a wedding, children....

Good things. Sensible things.

But for today – let's go happily berserk.

...

A happy and very, very LOUD birthday.

Only forgive the oldies if they sneak off into

another room.

Or street.

Or town.

...

<u>GO FOR IT!</u>

Make voyages. Attempt them. There's nothing else.

TENNESSEE WILLIAMS (1911-1983)

...

Time enough to be reasonable and sensible and
wary later on. But now – go for it.

PAM BROWN

...

Life is a great big canvas;
throw all the paint on it you can.

DANNY KAYE (1913-1987)

...

Jump into the middle of things, get your
hands dirty, fall flat on your face, and then
reach for the stars.

JOAN L. CURCIO

The world is so full of marvels to discover never let
a day pass without astonishing yourself.

PETER GRAY

...

That perfect job – fascinating work, charming
people, splendid salary, opportunities ahead,
chances to travel. It's out there somewhere. Go look
for it!! It's waiting for you.
The saddest thing in age is to realize you never
took the risk in youth that could have
changed your life.

PAM BROWN

...

The biggest human temptation is...
to settle for too little.

THOMAS MERTON

MY GIFTS TO YOU

I would tear down a star and put it into a smart
jewelry box if I could.
I would seal up love in a long thin bottle so
that you could sip it when ever it was needed
if I could.

ANNE SEXTON, IN A LETTER TO HER DAUGHTER

...

Love, peace and an enquiring mind.

That's what I wish for you....

Together with the ability to stand in other

people's shoes. And to laugh at yourself.

JONATHON A. HUGHES

...

What would I give you if I had the power? Not

great wealth – but enough to stave off anxiety and

to bring hope to the desperate. Not great beauty –

but a loving heart.

The chance to use your capabilities wisely and well

– to make a difference to the world,

and to delight you.

Perception to reveal to you the beauty that

surrounds you.

Courage to endure and grow.

Joy, contentment, love.

A life worth living.

PAM BROWN

...

TAKE COURAGE

Youth is the time for making mistakes.
So make them, with a happy heart!

PAM BROWN

...

My mother taught me to walk proud and
tall "as if the world was mine".

SOPHIA LOREN, b.1934

...

Each handicap is like a hurdle in a
steeplechase, and when you
ride up to it, if you throw your heart
over, the horse will go along too.

LAWRENCE BIXBY

...

Don't compromise yourself.

You're all you've got.

JANIS JOPLIN (1943-1970)

...

You have to accept whatever comes and the

only important thing is that you meet it

with courage and the best you have to give.

ELEANOR ROOSEVELT (1884-1962)

...

The best thing you can do is believe in

yourself. Don't be afraid to try.

Don't be afraid to fail.... Just dust yourself

off and try again....

JUDY GREEN HERBSTREIT,
FROM A LETTER TO HER DAUGHTER

...

ENJOY IT ALL...

Have fun! Enjoy the years that lie ahead.

Open your arms to all delight – of flowers and

music, every lovely thing. Of bold adventure and

astonishment. Of love.

Of friends you've yet to meet.

Be brave. Be curious. Be courteous.

Discover a wider world.

PAM BROWN

. . .

You already know love and learning, discovery,
adventure, joy and sorrow. But they have only been
a taste of life. Before you lie years far richer than
you can imagine. Accept them with joy.
Waste nothing – turn it all to good account.

PETER GRAY

...

Take time to be friendly –
It is the road to happiness.
Take time to dream –
It is hitching your wagon to a star.
Take time to love and to be loved –
It is the privilege of the gods.
Take time to look around –
It is too short a day to be selfish.
Take time to laugh –
It is the music of the soul.

OLD ENGLISH

...

COMING OF AGE

Just imagine the things you can do now
– *officially!*

PETER GRAY

. . .

You are free at last – not held by obligation.
Only by love.
Move out into the wider world. Treasure all that
life offers you in splendid pleasures and in
rich experience.
The world is your home.
All living things are your companions.
All people are your family.
... Enter into your kingdom.

PAM BROWN

. . .

DO IT NOW!

This is the time to do all the
things you will not dare to do in
later years.

…

Go to the ends of the earth
while you are young.
Learn new skills.
Discover wonders.
Don't put it off.
Or you'll find yourself out of puff
one day – only up to a slow
stroll round the park.

PAM BROWN

…

A lifetime is just long enough to do
something worth doing.
If you get going now.

CHARLOTTE GRAY

…

Don't be afraid your life will end; be afraid that it will never begin.

GRACE HANSEN

...

The years ahead seem endless

– but they're not.

Fill each day with joy and work and friendship. Remember, the millions who have said "One day I'll do it – when I've time. When I've money. When I've reached the top." And one day they may have the time and the money and be at the very top. And age will have stolen the longing – or the strength.

PAM BROWN

...

Stop sitting there with your hands folded looking on, doing nothing. Get into action and *live* this full and glorious life.

EILEEN CADDY

...

JUST BE YOU!

The challenge is to be yourself in a
world that is trying to make you like
everyone else.

RENEE LOOKS

. . .

Do not let people put you down.
Believe in yourself and stand for
yourself and trust yourself.

JACOB NEUSNER

. . .

This is your life, not someone else's. It
is your own feeling of what is
important, not what people will say.
Sooner or later, you are bound to
discover that you cannot please all of
the people around you all of the time.

ELEANOR ROOSEVELT (1884-1962),
FROM "YOU LEARN BY LIVING"

. . .

My mother's best advice to me was:
"Whatever you decide to do in life,
be sure that the joy of doing it does not
depend upon the applause of others,
because in the long run we are,
all of us, alone."

ALI MACGRAW

Follow what you love! ... Don't
deign to ask what "they" are looking
for out there.
Ask what you have inside. Follow
not your interests, which change, but
what you are and what you love, which
will and should not change.

GEORGIE ANNE GEYER

...

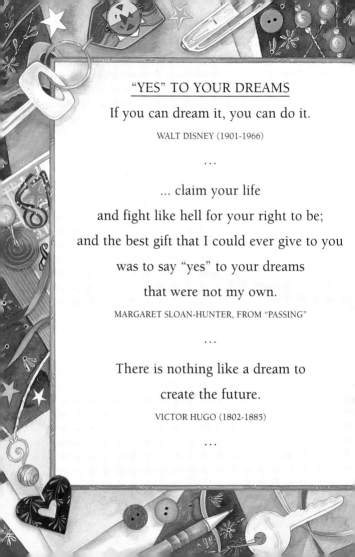

"YES" TO YOUR DREAMS

If you can dream it, you can do it.

WALT DISNEY (1901-1966)

. . .

... claim your life
and fight like hell for your right to be;
and the best gift that I could ever give to you
was to say "yes" to your dreams
that were not my own.

MARGARET SLOAN-HUNTER, FROM "PASSING"

. . .

There is nothing like a dream to
create the future.

VICTOR HUGO (1802-1885)

. . .

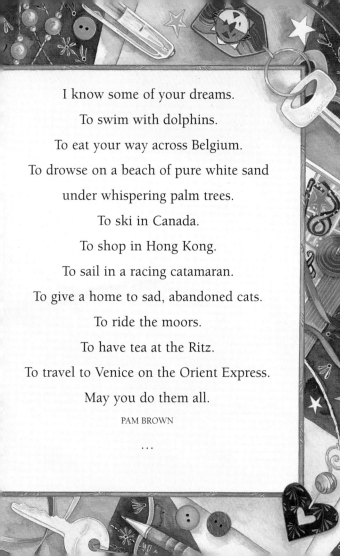

I know some of your dreams.

To swim with dolphins.

To eat your way across Belgium.

To drowse on a beach of pure white sand

under whispering palm trees.

To ski in Canada.

To shop in Hong Kong.

To sail in a racing catamaran.

To give a home to sad, abandoned cats.

To ride the moors.

To have tea at the Ritz.

To travel to Venice on the Orient Express.

May you do them all.

PAM BROWN

...

OUTWARD BOUND!

The world is out there – and if you work flat out you'll still only see a fraction of it before you fall off your perch. *So* – get out the books, get out the brochures, save your money, get your jobs, pack light – and *go*.

PETER GRAY

. . .

... you must always think well of yourself and realize your own worth. You are a pearl of great value. Don't ever forget those things, especially in your darkest moments.

TEENA, TO HER DAUGHTER KRISTI

. . .

You should want much for yourself: much love, stimulating experience, knowledge, giving others, and much outlet for your abilities. Don't settle for a little bit of any of these things.

NAN HUNT, FROM "BETWEEN OURSELVES"

. . .

Today is the end of the beginning. The rehearsal is over – the preparation for the real performance past. You have learned to learn. You have learned to love. Now to embark upon the real adventure.

…

The world is very big, the number of its people overwhelming. But listen for the laughter, the words of kindness. Let them give you courage – so that you in turn can bring to every life concern and gentleness, hope and delight.

…

MY WISHES FOR YOU

May you always find new paths to wander – new
adventures to dare, new chapters of life to open,
new changes to challenge you.

HELEN THOMSON, b.1943

...

Live in each season as it passes, breathe the air,
drink the drink, taste the fruit, and resign yourself
to the influences of each.

HENRY DAVID THOREAU (1817-1862)

May you *live* all the days of your life.

JONATHAN SWIFT (1667-1745)

. . .

I wish you the beauty of silence, the glory of sunlight, the mystery of darkness, the force of flame, the power of water, the sweetness of air, the quiet strength of earth, the love that lies at the very root of things. I wish you the wonder of living.

. . .

I wish you all good things – especially the gift of being able to let go. Learn from sorrow and mistakes. Then go on. And most of all I wish you courage. That usually takes care of everything else.

PAM BROWN

. . .

A little health, a little wealth, a little house and freedom. And at the end, a little friend, and little cause to need him.

AUTHOR UNKNOWN, FROM A NINETEENTH-CENTURY SAMPLER

. . .